How to Play Dizi, the Chinese Bamboo Flute – the Basic Skills

H.H. Lee

A guide to playing dizi, the Chinese bamboo flute at home by yourself

How to Play Dizi, the Chinese Bamboo Flute – the Basic Skills

ISBN: 9781549577536

First published on 29 August 2017

Edition 1.3 on 30 September 2019

Table of Contents

Preface

The dizi, also called Hengdi/横笛, is a Chinese transverse flute (horizontally held when played) usually carved with twelve holes. With a history of more than 8 000 years since the Neolithic Age, the dizi is one of the musical instruments indigenous to China. Known as the Chinese bamboo flute in the West, the dizi belongs to the blowing family[1] in the modern Chinese orchestra[2]. Popular for its portability and relatively low price, the dizi is playable in the forms of both solo and ensemble.

Members of the blowing family

Bangdi/梆笛 (left) and Qudi/曲笛 (right)

---

[1] The blowing family mainly consists of the bangdi/梆笛, qudi/曲笛, xindi/新笛; soprano, alto, tenor and bass shengs/笙; as well as soprano, alto, tenor and bass suonas /唢呐.

[2] The modern Chinese orchestra consists of four families, namely the bowing (bowed string), the plucking (plucked string), the blowing (wind) and the hitting (percussion).

Sheng/笙 (left) and Suona/嗩吶 (right)

The dizi is indispensable to the modern Chinese orchestra and plays a role similar to its western counterpart, the flute. Songs in different genres have emerged after the end of the Cultural Revolution, whilst the adaptation of foreign songs has brought continuous advances on playing techniques for the dizi.

In the following, I will show you how to play the dizi. Even if you are an amateur of Chinese music, you can still play some simple songs with enough efforts. Remember, practice makes perfect! But the first thing to do, doubtlessly, is to choose a dizi.

The Structure of the Dizi

An understanding of the dizi structure will help us to choose and play the instrument. In the following, the traditional six-holed bamboo flute will serve as the model for demonstration:

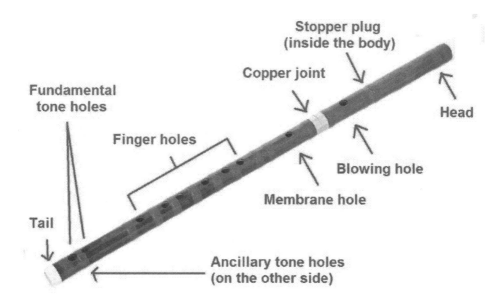

A schematic diagram is shown below for better illustration:

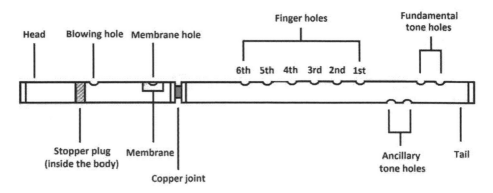

The parts of a dizi

The different parts of the dizi with their respective functions are described as follows:

Name	Description
Body	Dizis are mostly made of bamboo owing to its resonant nature and lower cost, though stone and jade are sometimes used. The body (except the head and tail) is painted with red lacquer and evenly wrapped with 21 to 24 rings of silk strings to prevent ruptures.
Head/ Tail	The two ends of the dizi are inlaid with ivory or cow bone for decoration.
Stopper plug	Made of cork, the stopper plug is imbedded into the body between the head and the blowing hole. It blocks the passage to the head, so air blown into the body can only leave in the opposite way (either through the finger holes or the fundamental tone holes). It also helps to tune the dizi.
Membrane	Made of reed film, the membrane resonates with the stationary waves generated in the body, whereby the dizi will produce clearer and brighter sounds.
Copper joint	Traditional dizis will be heated up after they have been blown for a while, which will raise their pitch unfortunately. To fix this problem, the body has been separated into two parts and connected by a copper joint, which can be positioned either between the blowing hole and the membrane hole, or between the membrane hole and the 6th hole. It helps to tune the dizi and separate the dizi into two parts, which facilitates transportation and storage.

Blowing hole	The hole through which air is blown into the body for vibrating the air inside and generating stationary waves.
Membrane hole	The hole onto which the membrane is affixed. Sounds can still be generated even without the presence of a membrane, yet the unique timbre of the dizi will be lost.
Finger holes	There are usually six (or even more in certain kinds of dizis) holes adjacently arranged on the body, and closing different holes each time can produce various notes. They are given an ordinal number (from first to sixth) to indicate their order, with the 1st hole near the tail and the 6th hole near the head.
Fundamental tone holes	The two fundamental tone holes can be used to adjust the fundamental tone of the dizi.
Ancillary tone holes	The two ancillary tone holes beneath the fundamental tone holes can be used to raise the pitch, as well as embellish and amplify the sound. Tassels can also be attached to them for decorative purposes.

Having understood the dizi structure, now let's learn to choose a dizi for ourselves.

How to Choose a Dizi

When choosing a dizi, we should pay heed to three criteria: material, craftsmanship and timbre. As its nickname "Chinese bamboo flute" implies, the quality of a dizi highly hinges upon the quality of the bamboo used. Various kinds of bamboos, such as *Bambusa multiplex*, *Pleioblastus amarus*, *Phyllostachys nigra*, *Fargesia semicoriacea* and *Phyllostachys bambusoides* can be used to make dizis, and what really matters is the age of the bamboo concerned.

Phyllostachys nigra (left) and *Phyllostachys bambusoides* (right)

New bamboo has a high water content, which will gradually dry out and collapse when it ages. This will lead to thin sound and unstable intonation. Yet, a bamboo that is too old, dried and thick will respond slowly with worse performance in the aspects of crispness and brightness. In view of these factors, we should choose old bamboo that has grown ideally for at least 3 years, which can somewhat be told from its color because a bamboo becomes darker in color when aging (from green to yellow). Some unscrupulous merchants smoke the bamboo to darken its color, but smoked bamboo will look obviously unnatural as compared with normal ones. As such, we should look for a dizi that is evenly colored in the first place.

The dizi is in fact a hollow tube. To avoid producing unpleasant sounds, the bamboo chosen should be tough, while its interior and exterior surfaces should be smooth and cylindrical in shape, even in thickness with the head slightly thicker than the tail. The interior surface, in particular, should be free of moth holes and cracks because such defects will undermine the quality of sounds generated.

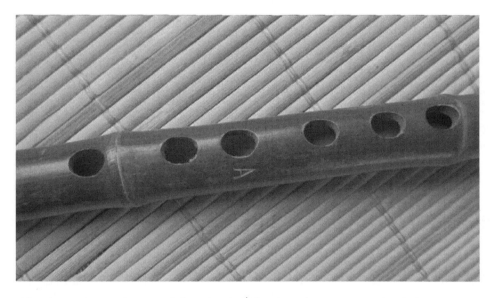

The above picture shows a dizi made of old bamboo that appears to be darker in color

Next, we need to examine the craftsmanship. We should avoid dizis with heavy paint coating on both interior and exterior surfaces, for this will hinder our identification of cracks and the "respiration" of the dizi. The blowing hole, membrane hole and finger holes should all be appropriately carved, so that they are glossy without hair. As per the general standards, the blowing hole should be round in shape; the membrane hole more or less oval in shape; and the finger holes totally oval in shape. All of the holes should be carved from outside at an angle, by which they gradually become bigger from the exterior to interior.

Finally, we need to check the timbre.   Before checking for the intonation, we have to blow the dizi first to warm it, as the pitch will rise with temperature inside the tube.   Thereafter, we can start with the following notes to see whether their pitches are correct: the groups of solfeggi " 5̣ "/" 5 "/" 5̇ ", then " 1 "/" 1̇ ", " 4 "/" 4̇ " and " 6 "/" 6̇ " that are octaves; subsequently, those pairs of solfeggi " 2 "/" 5 ", " 3 "/" 6 " " 1 "/" 4 ", " 7 "/" 3 ", " 6̣ "/" 2 " and " 5̣ "/" 1 " that are a perfect fourth or perfect fifth apart in interval; the scale within the 1st octave in the ascending order; and eventually the overtones [3] (which are quite difficult for an amateur to produce, so it is advisable to have an experienced player to accompany you when choosing a dizi).

By producing a long tone for each note, we can ascertain the minimum amount of air blown into the dizi to maintain their pitches.   With an appropriate beam of blowing air, no hissing noise should be heard; the highest notes should be clear and even, while the lowest notes should be solid and full.   We can bring along a tuner to assist in the checking process, but should never produce the notes in an attempt to suit the tuner.   This is because the finger holes of the dizi is not carved on the basis of equal temperament, but rather on Pythagorean tuning[4].   If we rely on the tuner too much to tune the dizi, its resulting timbre will lack the charisma and style of Chinese music.

---

[3]   Tones with frequencies as integer multiples (2, 3, 4, 5...) of the fundamental frequency are called overtones.   The fundamental frequency is the frequency of the fundamental tone, which is the lowest note a musical instrument that can produce.

[4]   The Pythagorean tuning is a system of musical tuning in which the frequency ratios of all intervals are based on the ratio 3:2.

The membrane is an essential part of the dizi, which determines the timbre of a dizi to a large extent. Therefore, it is important to know how to choose a good membrane too.

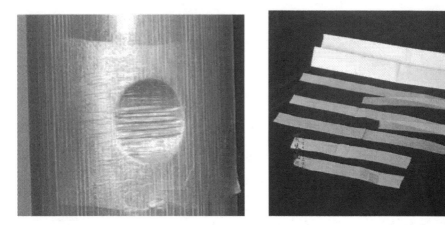

A membrane affixed onto the membrane hole   Membranes sold in the market

The membrane, called dimo/笛膜 in Chinese, can be made of sheep casings, bamboo or reed. The sheep casings-typed membrane is very thin, but the timbre is dull; the bamboo-typed membrane has a bright timbre, but it lacks resilience and will break easily when we blow strongly. The reed-typed membrane combines both of their strengths and is thus widely employed nowadays.

A good membrane depends on two factors: age and width. An old membrane appears to be yellowish, wide and thick, whereas a new membrane appears to be whitish, narrow and thin. An old membrane makes dull and hard sounds, while a new membrane makes rustling noises and is prone to breakage. In this connection, neither of them is deemed suitable. We have to strike a balance between the old and new membranes such that the age and width factors can be satisfied at the same time; in other words, an ideal membrane should be thin but elastic, transparent and shiny in appearance.

If the dizi obtained from a music store or elsewhere does not have a membrane, we can affix one to it by taking the following steps:

Step 1

Step 2

Wash the hands thoroughly first to prevent dirt and dust from sticking onto the new membrane. Check the membrane hole to remove any remnants of the old membrane.

New membranes available in the market look like adhesive tapes. Take out a strip of membrane from the packaging.

Step 3

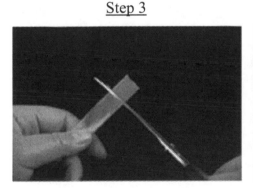

Step 4

Cut the strip with a pair of scissors to obtain a square piece that is 1.5 to 2 times in width of the membrane hole.

As the membrane is a two-layered tube, cut and make it into a single-layered piece.

12

Step 5

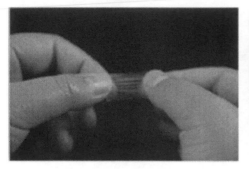

Gently stretch the membrane for several times to make creases evenly thereon, which can facilitate vibrations later. Grip the longitudinal sides of the membrane such that the natural veins of the membrane become perpendicular to the creases.

Step 6

Afterwards, dip some Donkey-hide gelatin (or dried bulb of hyacinth orchid with plain water) around the membrane hole. Remove any excess glue with our little finger.

Step 7

Stick the membrane on its hole horizontally (perpendicular to the vein) if it is young to resist shock and breakage, or vertically (parallel to the vein) if is old to enhance synchronized vibrations.

Step 8

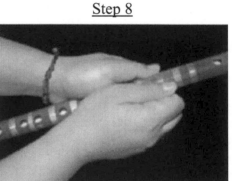

Gently stretch the membrane for several times again. By doing so, the creases on the membrane should be dense at the center and gradually scarce at the periphery.

The membrane has been successfully affixed onto the membrane hole.

(Remarks: the pictures above are extracted from the following blog http://blog.sina.com.cn/u/1014430442, where a lot of information about the dizi in simplified Chinese can be found.)

If the membrane is stuck too tightly, the sounds produced will not be bright and crisp; on the contrary, if the membrane is stuck too loosely, the sounds produced will become hoarse and it will be difficult to produce high notes. Under both circumstances, we can soften the edges of the membrane with a few drops of water, and then stretch the membrane if it is too loose, or press the center of the membrane if it is too tight. Bear in mind that we must not dampen the membrane directly at the center, which will ruin it immediately.

At last, we need to decide on the type of dizis that we are going to play. As mentioned before, there are basically three types of dizi, namely the bangdi, qudi and xindi. The xindi, also called "eleven-holed di" (due to the addition of five more finger holes), was developed on the basis of equal temperament.

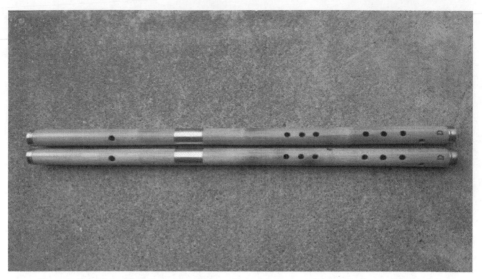

Two D-key xindis (please note that there is no membrane hole on the body)

Designed by DING Silin/丁西林 (1893-1974) in the 1930s to resolve the problem in producing semitones and the trouble with changing different dizis (the reason will be explained later), the xindi has its membrane removed and thus its timbre is not so bright and crisp as traditional dizis. Coupled with its complicated fingering arrangements, the xindi is not recommended for beginners.

On the other hand, the bangdi and qudi are the major kinds of dizis played today, which share several similarities and differences in their structures:

Bangdis are popular in the Northern China, and mainly used in the accompaniment of *bangzi* operas. Compared with qudis, bangdis are shorter, higher in pitch and their timbre is brighter. Bangdis' ornamentations are specialized in the motions of the tongue.

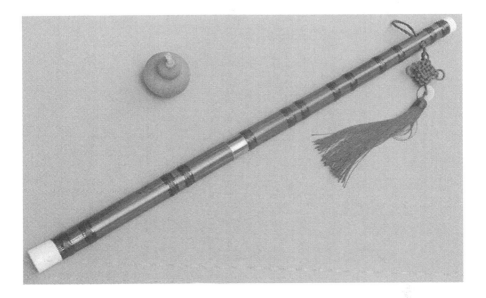

Qudis are popular in the Southern China, and mainly used in the accompaniment of *kunqu* operas and *Jiangnan sizhu*. Compared with bangdis, qudis are longer and mellower in tone. Qudis' ornamentations are specialized in the control of blowing air.

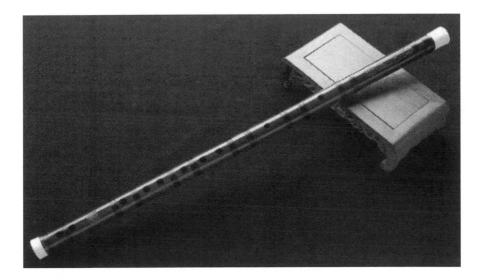

The bangdi and qudi both have 6 finger holes, and the note of the

3rd hole (i.e. what we hear when the 1st, 2nd and 3rd holes are opened while the 4th, 5th and 6th holes are closed) defines the key of the dizi. For instance, if a D note is produced in this fingering arrangement, the dizi concerned will be a D-key dizi and a small letter "D" will be marked beside the 3rd hole. In this respect, there are a total of 7 dizis corresponding to the keys A, B, C, D, E, F and G, which form the common set found in the market (there is also a set of 12 dizis that contains the remaining A♭, B♭, D♭, E♭, and G♭ keys on top of the seven neutral keys).

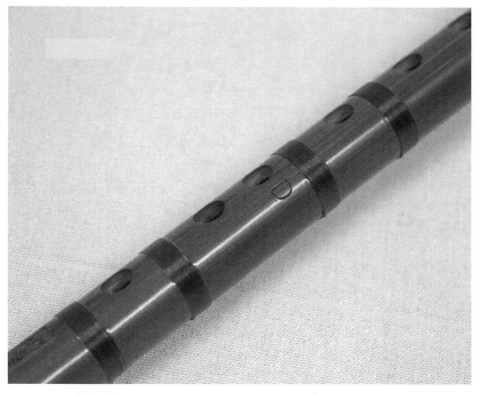

A small letter "D" is clearly carved next to the 3rd hole of a D-key qudi

Amateurs can either pick a bangdi or a qudi, and the common ones in use are as follows:

The A-key bangdis (44.5 cm in length, with a range from E4 to A6);

the G-key bangdis (48 cm in length, with a range from D4 to G6);

the F-key bangdis (52 cm in length, with a range from C4 to F6);

the E-key qudis (56 cm in length, with a range from B3 to E6);

the D-key qudis (60 cm in length, with a range from A3 to D6); and

the C-key qudis (67 cm in length, with a range from G3 to C6).

For the purpose of illustration, the D-key qudi will serve as the model for demonstration in the following chapters of this book.

How to Play the Dizi

The posture

A correct posture is the cornerstone of playing the dizi. To play the dizi, we can either stand up or sit on a chair, but we usually stand up during practices or performing solo on stage, so let's talk about the standing posture first.

For the standing posture, we have to stand still with our toes pointing outwards. If the tail of the dizi inclines to the left, our right foot, which is also the center of gravity at the same time, should be in front of our left foot, and vice versa. Keep our body straight (especially the upper parts). Open our arms at an angle of 45° and hold the dizi in a plane so that our mouth is perpendicular to the blowing hole.

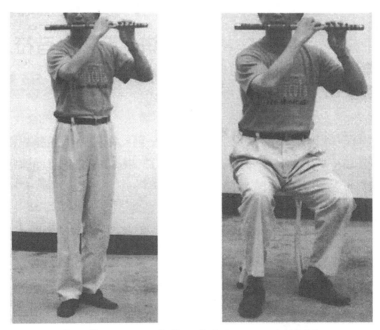

Standing posture (left) and sitting posture (right)

As for the sitting posture, all the above hold true except that we usually open rather than cross our legs, by which we can sit firmly on the chair and will not affect our breathing.

The fingers

Thereafter, we have to learn how to hold the dizi and press its holes.

We can hold the dizi to the left or to the right, but it is advisable to hold the dizi to the right in conformity with the international standards. When pressing the finger holes, we can either use the 1st joints of our fingers (between the distal phalanx and the middle phalanx) or the fingertips. In fact, we only play extra-large or extra-small dizis with our fingertips to allow greater flexibility; otherwise, we normally press the finger holes with the 1st joints of our fingers as follows:

Right ring finger: 1st hole;
Right middle finger: 2nd hole;
Right index finger: 3rd hole;
Right thumb: the opposite side between the 2nd and 3rd holes;
Right little finger: placed on the dizi gently.

Left ringer finger: 4th hole;
Left middle finger: 5th hole;
Left index finger: 6th hole;
Left thumb: beneath the space between the 6th hole and membrane hole;
Left little finger: placed on the dizi gently.

The above picture shows how we hold the dizi with our fingers

The breathing method

The thoracoabdominal breathing method (i.e. using both of the chest and abdomen to breathe) is the most suitable method for playing the dizi. We can practice deep breathing until we can produce steady, slow and long breaths. If you find it difficult, you can begin with using the abdomen only: after exhaling all the air, fasten the chest with a belt and breathe with the abdomen. Breathe in air quickly and out slowly, during which you will feel cool in the throat. When blowing out air, we can mimic the way dogs gasping for air in the summer, but just we don't put our tongue out.

During the performance, there are three types of blowing ways, viz.:

1) Slow blowing: the speed of airflow is slow and steady, with a thick beam of air. The upper and lower lips relax and we breathe leisurely.

2) Fast blowing: the speed of airflow is fast and strong, with a thin beam of air. The upper and lower lips contract and we breathe hurriedly.

3) Overblowing: the speed of airflow is fast and explosive, with a negligible beam of air. The upper and lower lips contract and we breathe exaggeratedly.

<u>The mouth</u>

We have to blow the dizi with the proper embouchure [5], and the prerequisite is to relax our mouth and lips as much as possible. The upper and lower lips form an oval shape as if we were smiling, i.e. our lip muscles adhere to the gum naturally, while the two sides of our mouth contract.

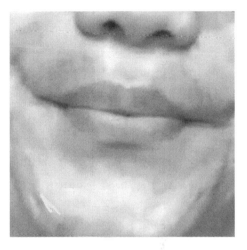

Meanwhile, our mouth slightly opens whereas the tongue remains calm. Then, gently position our mouth toward the blowing hole with our tongue covering the teeth on the lower jaw, where our lower lip adheres to the periphery of the blowing hole and covers 1/4 of it. At the same time, we can blow air into the hole steadily with concentration, and let the lip muscles move with the airflow.

---

[5] The embouchure is the oval gap formed by the upper and lower lips through which the airflow passes.

To ensure the effectiveness of the embouchure, NEVER:

1) Blow up the cheek;
2) Pout;
3) Leak out air at the corners of the mouth; and
4) Protrude either of the upper or lower lip.

When low notes are produced, our facial and lip muscles contract to expand the embouchure and the airflow becomes weaker. On the contrary, our facial and lip muscles relax to constrict the embouchure and the airflow becomes stronger when high notes are produced.

Afterwards, we can start playing simple songs, though beforehand we have to learn to read the **numbered musical notation**, which is widely adopted in Chinese sheet music.

The Numbered Music Notation

The sheet music of the famous English folk song, *Scarborough Fair*, is attached below for demonstrating how to read and interpret sheet music recorded in the numbered music notation:

Scarborough fair

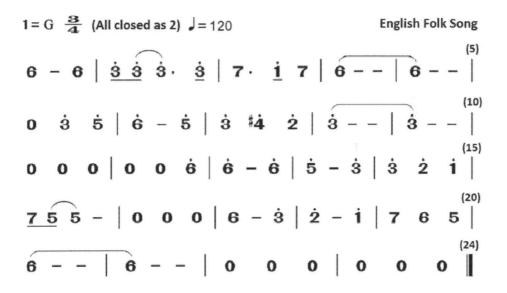

The numbered music notation is based on the French Galin-Paris-Chevé system and known as *jianpu*/簡譜 in China. The sheet music for all Chinese musical instruments (including the dizi) is written in this notation, so we must learn to read it.

General principles

The numbered music notation gets its name because it uses numbers (0 – 7) to represent musical notes, but the numbers indeed tally with the solfeggi directly:

1 = do; 2 = re; 3 = mi; 4 = fa; 5 = sol; 6 = la, 7 = si/ti; and 0 = a rest irrespective of the key signatures of the sheet music.

Now let's examine the above sheet music part by part in detail.

1) The name of the song "*Scarborough Fair*" is located at the top;

2) The origin (/composer/ arranger) of the song "*English Folk Song*" is located at the top-right corner;

3) The key signature (1 = G), time signature (3/4) and tempo ($\flat$ = 120) of the song are all located at the top-left corner;

4) The small number inside the bracket indicates the current bar number (the 5th, 10th, 15th, 20th and 24th bars, all of which are the last bar of every line in this song, are marked accordingly); and

5) The song ends in Bar 24. The bars are usually arranged in the order of a number's multiple (like there are 5 bars per line in this sheet music except the 5th line), but the actual arrangement depends on the number of notes present within a bar. More notes will lead to fewer bars per line. The following signs carry the same meaning in both staff and numbered music notations:

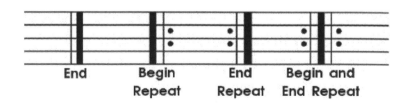

End   Begin   End   Begin and
          Repeat   Repeat End Repeat

The key signature

The key signature is indicated by the expression $1 = X$ for majors and $6 = X$ for minors, though the minor notation is never used as far as I have observed.   This song is in G major as indicated by $1 = G$.

The phrase (all closed as 2) beside the time signature is actually a literal translation of the Chinese phrase （筒音／全按作 2）.   The Chinese term " 筒 音 " means the fundamental tone of the dizi, which is produced by blowing it with all the six finger holes covered with our fingers.   By treating the fundamental tone as the solfeggio "2" (re), we can play this song by varying the fingering combination.   The relationship between the fundamental tone and the key signature will be explained later.

The octaves are represented by adding a dot above or below the number. A dot below the number lowers the note by an octave, whereas a dot above the number raises the note by an octave.   For example, $\dot{1}$ is at an octave higher than 1 whereas $\,\underset{.}{1}$ is at an octave lower than 1 .

The sharp (♯) sign raises the note by a semi-tone and the flat (♭) sign lowers the note by a semi-tone, whereas the natural (♮) sign neutralizes any sharps or flats from preceding notes or the key signature.

The time signature

The time signature is represented by fractions such as 2/4, 4/4, 6/8... which mean that there are 2 quarter notes per bar, 4 quarter notes per bar and 6 eighth notes per bar respectively.   In this song, there are 3 quarter notes per bar as indicated by the fraction 3/4.

The tempo

The tempo, if any, will be written next to the time signature in the form of $\flat = X$, which means that there are X quarter notes per minute. In this song, $\flat = 120$ means that there are 120 quarter notes per minute. Sometimes, you may find a symbol ↮, which means "Ad libitum" (as you desire). Nonetheless, the tempo will vary as per the requirements of individual songs.

The note value

Underlined notes (like the solfeggio " $\underline{1}$ " in Bar 3) will have their lengths decreased by half per underline they have. On the contrary, notes followed by a dot (also the solfeggio " $7 \cdot$ " in Bar 3) will have their lengths increased by half. If they are followed by a hyphen (like the solfeggio " 6- " in Bar 5) instead of a dot, their lengths will be doubled.

Though absent in the above sheet music, dynamics (*p, f, mf, mp, ff, pp*), hairline crescendos and diminuendos will be written below the notes if necessary.

There are also dizi-specific marks that instruct us how to play the notes correctly. Musical symbols commonly found in dizi sheet music are tabulated below (certain skills are transliterated into their *pinyin* for the sake of faithfulness):

Symbol	Name	Meaning
⌒	Legato	Maintain continuous airflow for all linked notes (the first note can be played with light tonguing)
–	Tenuto	Hold the specified note its full length
>	Accent	Blow the dizi strongly for the specified note
V	Breath	Take a breath at where it is indicated
T or ▼	Tonguing	Add a rest of equal length after each note by articulating the "T" consonant
TK	Double tonguing	Add a rest of equal length after each note by articulating the "TK" consonants
TTK/ TKT	Triple tonguing	Add a rest of equal length after each note by articulating the "TTK" or "TKT" consonants
◉	Light tonguing	Produce a clear and continuous note, similar to the pronunciation of the "she" sound
↗ or ↘	Glissando (up or down)	Glide upward to a note from the original note, or downward from the original note to another note
tr	Trill	Alternate the main note with another note rapidly for multiple times
乇	Flying fingers	Fingers slide over their holes swiftly in a sideways direction

$\diagup$ or $\diagdown$	Run (up or down)	Play the note up to the octave above, or down to the octave below
⅃	*Duoyin*	Glide fiercely from a note to another note
又	*Dieyin*	Play the grace note and quickly shift to the main note, with all the neutral notes bounded by them heard vaguely
扌 or Ｔ	*Dayin*	Hit the finger hole of the next lower note to produce an extra short note after the main note
$\frac{(4)}{\mathstrut\,}$	*Zengyin*	Add a short note (lower or higher by several intervals) after the main note, usually at the end of a sentence
∼∼∼	Vibrato (blowing)	Generate a wave-like note by using the diaphragm, and muscles of the chest and abdomen
⊖	Vibrato (fingering)	Generate a wave-like note by virtually shaking the finger
○	Harmonic	Produce an overtone by blowing the note in accordance with the Pythagorean tuning
⦿→	*Rouyin*	Gently vibrate the finger in the vertical or horizontal plane before covering the hole
⁎	Flutter tonguing	Vibrate the tip of the tongue to make characteristic sounds

29

⊗	Throat sound	Vibrate the palatine uvula to make characteristic sounds
Ⓥ	Circular breathing	Blow the dizi and breathe simultaneously
▽⃝	Circular tonguing	Perform tonguing and breathe simultaneously

The advanced skills introduced in this table, in particular harmonic, *rouyin*, flutter tonguing, circular breathing and circular tonguing, will not be discussed now. In the meantime, if you are able to read the above sheet music without any difficulties, we can move on to the next stage to begin practicing with the fingering chart.

The Key Signatures of the Dizi

The fingering chart of a six-holed D-key dizi is shown below:

Fingering hole / Blowing way	6th hole	5th hole	4th hole	3rd hole	2nd hole	1st hole	1=D (All closed as 5)	1=G (All closed as 2)	1=A (All closed as 1)	1=C (All closed as 6)	1=F (All closed as 3)
Slow blowing	●	●	●	●	●	●	5	2	1	6	3
	●	●	●	●	●	◐	#5	#2	#1	#6	4
	●	●	●	●	●	○	6	3	2	7	#4
	●	●	●	●	◐	○	7	4	#3	1	5
	●	●	●	●	○	○	7	#4	3	#1	#5
	●	●	●	○	○	○	1	5	4	2	6
	●	●	◐	○	○	○	#1	#5	#4	#2	#6
	●	○	●	●	○	○	2	6	5	3	7
	●	○	○	○	○	○	#2	#6	#5	#4	1
	○	●	●	○	○	○	#3	7	6	5	#1
	◐	○	○	○	○	○	4	1	7	5	2
	○	○	○	○	○	○	#4	#1	7	#5	#2
Fast blowing	○	●	●	●	●	●	5	2	#1	6	3
	●	●	●	●	●	◐	#5	#2	#1	7	4
	●	●	●	●	●	○	6	3	2	1	#4
	●	●	●	●	◐	○	7	#3	#2	#1	5
	●	●	●	●	○	○	7	4	3	2	#5
	●	●	●	○	○	○	1	5	4	3	6
	●	●	○	○	○	○	#1	#5	#4	#3	#6
	●	○	○	○	○	○	2	6	5	4	7
	○	●	●	●	●	○	1	#5	#4	#3	#6
	◐	○	○	○	○	○	#4	#1	7	#5	#2
	○	○	○	●	◐	○	#4	#1	7	#5	#2
	○	●	●	●	●	●	4	1	7	5	2
	○	●	●	○	○	○					
	●	●	●	◐	●	◐	#5	#2	#1	#6	#2
	●	●	●	○	●	○	5	2	1	6	3
	●	◐	●	○	◐	◐	#5	#6	#1	#6	4
	●	○	●	●	●	○	7	4	2	3	#4
	●	○	○	●	◐	○	4	#2	#2	4	5
	●	○	●	●	○	●	7	3	3	#4	#5
	○	○	●	○	●	●	1	5	4	2	6

Remarks: " ● " as closed ; " ○ " as opened ; " ◐ " as half-closed

The fingering chart of the dizi has been traditionally marked in the *Gongche* notation (工尺譜), which uses Chinese characters to represent musical notes. However, the *Gongche* notation is mainly restricted to Chinese operas now, so I will illustrate the fingering chart with the aid of the numbered musical notation (both systems are based on the solfeggi but not actual musical notes).

When we blow air into the blowing hole, stationary waves will be generated inside the dizi. The pitch of the note we play depends on the frequency of the stationary waves, which is in turn subject to the acoustic length of the dizi. When all finger holes are closed, air will leave through the fundamental tone holes, whereby the dizi will produce the fundamental tone. By covering different finger holes in accordance with the fingering chart, air will leave through the 1st, 2nd, 3rd, 4th, 5th and 6th holes respectively (the acoustic length will gradually diminish in this order). As a result, the wavelength of the stationary waves inside the dizi will become shorter, whereas the pitch of the note will become higher.

The above fingering chart is valid for 6 holed-dizis in all keys, except that the 1 = X (key signature) on the leftmost column will change according to the key of the dizi. When applying the above chart, we have to remember that the solfeggi remain unchanged but the actual musical notes will vary depending on the key of the dizi. Take the G-key dizi as an example (hereinafter "0th" means that all the six holes are closed while "3rd" stands for the 3rd hole. Bear in mind that the note produced by the 3rd hole will always be **G natural** in this case, so NO accidentals can be added to the G note):

When treating the fundamental solfeggio as " 5̣ ", 1 = G.

Hole	0th	/	/	3rd	/	/	/	/
Note	D	E	F♯	G	A	B	C	D
Solfeggio	5̣	6̣	7̣	1	2	3	4	5

When treating the fundamental solfeggio as " 2̣ ", 1 = C.

Hole	0th	/	/	3rd	/	/	/	/
Note	D	E	F	G	A	B	C	D
Solfeggio	2̣	3̣	4̣	5̣	6̣	7̣	1	2

When treating the fundamental solfeggio as " 1 ", 1 = D.

Hole	0th	/	/	3rd	/	/	/	/
Note	D	E	F♯	G	A	B	C♯	D
Solfeggio	1	2	3	4	5	6	7	i

When treating the fundamental solfeggio as " 6̣ ", 1 = F.

Hole	0th	/	/	3rd	/	/	/	/
Note	D	E	F	G	A	B♭	C	D
Solfeggio	6̣	7̣	1	2	3	4	5	6

When treating the fundamental solfeggio as " 3̣ ", 1 = B♭.

Hole	0th	/	/	3rd	/	/	/	/
Note	D	E♭	F	G	A	B♭	C	D
Solfeggio	3̣	4̣	5̣	6̣	7̣	1	2	3

For the sake of simplicity, the key signatures with regard to different sets of fundamental tones and keys of the dizi are tabulated as follows:

Key of the dizi	Fundamental tone of the dizi											
	5	#5	6	#6	7	1	#1	2	#2	3	4	#4
C	C	B	Bb	A	Ab	G	Gb	F	E	Eb	D	Db
Db	Db	C	B	Bb	A	Ab	G	Gb	F	E	Eb	D
D	D	Db	C	B	Bb	A	Ab	G	Gb	F	E	Eb
Eb	Eb	D	Db	C	B	Bb	A	Ab	G	Gb	F	E
E	E	Eb	D	Db	C	B	Bb	A	Ab	G	Gb	F
F	F	E	Eb	D	Db	C	B	Bb	A	Ab	G	Gb
Gb	Gb	F	E	Eb	D	Db	C	B	Bb	A	Ab	G
G	G	Gb	F	E	Eb	D	Db	C	B	Bb	A	Ab
Ab	Ab	G	Gb	F	E	Eb	D	Db	C	B	Bb	A
A	A	Ab	G	Gb	F	E	Eb	D	Db	C	B	Bb
Bb	Bb	A	Ab	G	Gb	F	E	Eb	D	Db	C	B
B	B	Bb	A	Ab	G	Gb	F	E	Eb	D	Db	C

For instance, when we treat the fundamental solfeggio of a D-key dizi as " **1** ", the resulting key signature will be A major consequently. In other words, if we want to play A major with a D-key dizi, we have to treat the fundamental solfeggio as " **1** ". Under normal circumstances, the sheet music will tell us the fundamental tone and the type of dizi used in addition to the key signature of the song, but this is not guaranteed. If either one is missing, we can deduce it with the help of the above table.

To familiarize ourselves with this table, we shall do a quiz:
1. To play C major with a F-key bangdi, what should the fundamental solfeggio be treated?
2. To play F major with a D-key qudi, what should the fundamental solfeggio be treated?

3. To play F major with a G-key bangdi, what should the fundamental solfeggio be treated?

4. To play C major with a C-key qudi, what should the fundamental solfeggio be treated?

5. To play A major with a E-key qudi, what should the fundamental solfeggio be treated?

(The answers can be found on Page 46.)

Theoretically by treating the fundamental tone as different solfeggi, all the 12 majors can be played with one single bangdi/ qudi. However, pragmatically we only treat the fundamental tone as the solfeggi " 5 ", " 6 ", " 1 ", " 2 " and " 3 " (as the dizi is diatonic in nature), and it is already good enough for an amateur to know only two of them, i.e. by treating the fundamental tone as the solfeggi " 5 " and " 2 ", namely *Xiao Gong Diao*/小工調 and *Zheng Gong Diao*/正宮調 respectively in the traditional *Gongche* notation[6]. Let's apply the fingering chart above with a D-key qudi (range from A3 to D6) under the *Xiao Gong Diao*/小工調, in which the fundamental solfeggio is treated as " 5 ":

---

[6] The seven keys of the *Gongche* notation (工尺七調) include

Name	Fundamental tone in terms of solfeggio	Corresponding Key in Modern Western Music
Xiao Gong Diao/小工調	5	D
Zheng Gong Diao/正宮調	2	G
Liu Zi Diao/六字調	3	F
Chi Zi Diao/尺字調	6	C
Fan Zi Diao/凡字調	4	Eb
Yi Zi Diao/乙字調	1	A
Shang Zi Diao/上字調	7	Bb

In the following diagrams, "B" stands for the blowing hole; "M" stands for the membrane hole; whereas "1", "2", "3", "4", "5" and "6" stands for the 1st, 2nd, 3rd, 4th, 5th and 6th holes respectively (a black semicircle means that the hole is closed; a white semicircle means that the hole is opened; whereas a black-and-white semicircle means that the hole is half-closed).

<u>With slow blowing</u>

Closing all the six holes will produce the A3 note, which corresponds to the solfeggio " ⁵ ";

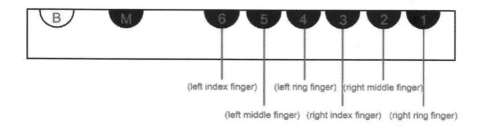

Closing all except the 1st hole will produce the B3 note, which corresponds to the solfeggio " ⁶ ";

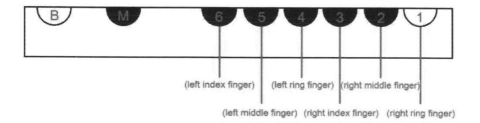

Closing all but the 1st and 2nd holes will produce the C♯4 note, which corresponds to the solfeggio " ⁷ ";

36

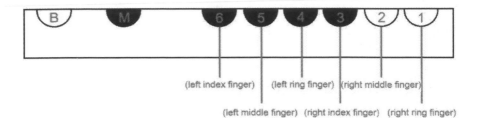

Closing half of the holes (4th, 5th and 6th) will produce the D4 note, which corresponds to the solfeggio " **1** " (this explains why the dizi in question is a D-key dizi);

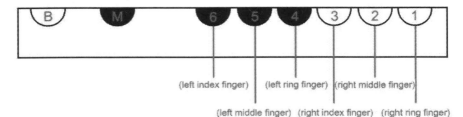

Closing the 5th and 6th holes will produce the E4 note, which corresponds to the solfeggio " **2** ";

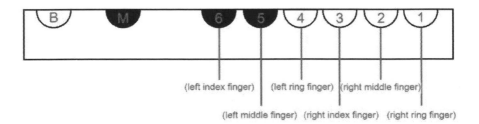

Closing the 6th hole only will produce the F♯4 note, which corresponds to the solfeggio " **3** ";

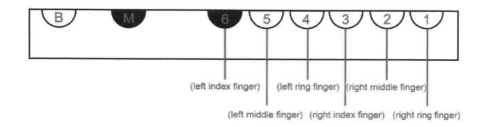

(left index finger)   (left ring finger)   (right middle finger)

(left middle finger)   (right index finger)   (right ring finger)

Closing half of the 6th hole will produce the G4 note, which corresponds to the solfeggio " 4 "; and

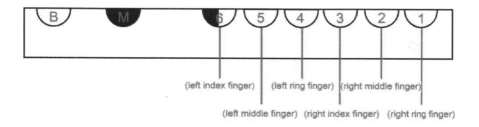

(left index finger)   (left ring finger)   (right middle finger)

(left middle finger)   (right index finger)   (right ring finger)

With fast blowing

Closing all except the 6th hole will produce the A4 note, which corresponds to the solfeggio " 5 ".

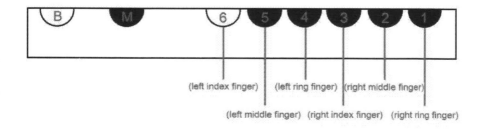

(left index finger)   (left ring finger)   (right middle finger)

(left middle finger)   (right index finger)   (right ring finger)

We have hereby completed the octave from A3 to A4, and the other octaves will follow the patterns shown in the latter half of the fingering chart.

For easy reference, I also attach herewith the fingering charts of F-key and G-key bangdis as well as C-key and E-key qudis, in case you cannot figure out the mechanism for applying the table with respect to the relationship between the fundamental tones and keys of the dizi.

The fingering chart of a six-holed F-key dizi:

Column key for holes — "●" = closed, "○" = opened, "◑" = half-closed.

Slow blowing

1st hole	2nd hole	3rd hole	4th hole	5th hole	6th hole	1=F	1=Bb	1=C	1=Eb	1=Ab
●	●	●	●	●	●	5	2	1	6	3
◑	●	●	●	●	●	#5	#2	#1	#6	4
○	●	●	●	●	●	6	3	2	7	#4
○	◑	●	●	●	●	♭7	4	♭3	1	5
○	○	●	●	●	●	7	#4	3	#1	#5
○	○	○	●	●	●	1	5	4	2	6
○	○	○	◑	●	●	#1	#5	#4	#2	#6
○	○	○	○	●	●	2	6	5	3	7
○	○	●	●	○	●	♭3	♭7	♭6	4	1
○	○	○	○	○	●	3	7	6	#4	#1
○	○	○	●	●	○	4	1	7	5	2
○	○	○	○	○	◑					
○	○	○	○	○	○	#4	#1	♭7	#5	#2

Fast blowing

1st hole	2nd hole	3rd hole	4th hole	5th hole	6th hole	1=F	1=Bb	1=C	1=Eb	1=Ab
●	●	●	●	●	○	5	2	1	6	3
◑	●	●	●	●	●	#5	#2	#1	♭7	4
○	●	●	●	●	●	6	3	2	7	#4
○	◑	●	●	●	●	♭7	4	♭3	1	5
○	○	●	●	●	●	7	#4	3	#1	#5
○	○	○	●	●	●	1	5	4	2	6
○	○	○	◑	●	●	#1	#5	#4	#2	#6
○	○	○	○	●	●	2	6	5	3	7
○	○	○	○	◑	●	♭3	♭7	♭6	4	1
○	○	○	○	○	●	3	7	6	#4	#1
●	●	●	●	●	○	4	1	7	5	2
○	○	○	○	○	◑					
○	◑	●	○	○	○	#4	#1	♭7	#5	#2
●	●	●	●	●	○	5	2	1	6	3
○	○	○	●	●	○	#5	#2	#1	♭7	4
◑	●	●	◑	●	●	6	3	2	7	#4
○	●	●	○	●	●	♭7	4	♭3	1	5
●	●	●	●	○	●	7	#4	3	#1	#5
●	○	●	●	○	●	1	5	4	2	6
○	◑	●	○	●	●	♭7	4	♭3	1	5
●	●	●	●	○	●	7	#4	3	#1	#5
●	○	●	●	○	●					
○	○	○	●	○	●	1	5	4	2	6

Remarks: "●" as closed; "○" as opened; "◑" as half-closed

1=F — All closed as 5
1=Bb — All closed as 2
1=C — All closed as 1
1=Eb — All closed as 6
1=Ab — All closed as 3

The fingering chart of a six-holed G-key dizi:

Blowing way	1st hole	2nd hole	3rd hole	4th hole	5th hole	6th hole	1 = G	1 = C	1 = D	1 = F	1 = Bb
Slow blowing	●	●	●	●	●	●	5̣	2	1	6̣	3
	◐	●	●	●	●	●	#5̣	#2	#1	b7̣	4
	○	●	●	●	●	●	6̣	3	2	7̣	#4
	○	◐	●	●	●	●	b7̣	4	b3	1	5
	○	○	●	●	●	●	7̣	#4	3	#1	#5
	○	○	○	●	●	●	1	5	4	2	6
	○	○	○	◐	●	●	#1	#5	#4	#2	#6
	○	○	○	○	●	●	2	6	5	3	7
	○	○	○	○	◐	●	b3	b7	b6	4	1̇
	○	○	○	○	○	●	3	7	6	#4	#1̇
	○	○	○	○	○	○	4	1̇	b7	5	2̇
	○	○	○	○	○	◐					
Fast blowing	●	○	○	○	○	○	#4	#1̇	7	#5	#2̇
	●	●	●	●	●	●	5	2̇	1̇	6	3̇
	◐	●	●	●	●	●	#5	#2̇	#1̇	b7	4̇
	○	●	●	●	●	●	6	3̇	2̇	7	#4̇
	○	◐	●	●	●	●	b7	4̇	b3̇	1̇	5̇
	○	○	●	●	●	●	7	#4̇	3̇	#1̇	#5̇
	○	○	○	●	●	●	1̇	5̇	4̇	2̇	6̇
	○	○	○	◐	●	●	#1̇	#5̇	#4̇	#2̇	#6̇
	○	○	○	○	●	●	2̇	6̇	5̇	3̇	7̇
	○	○	○	○	◐	●	b3̇	b7̇	b6̇	4̇	1̈
	○	○	○	○	○	●	3̇	7̇	6̇	#4̇	#1̈
	○	○	○	○	○	○	4̇	1̈	b7̇	5̇	2̈
	○	○	○	○	○	◐					
	●	○	○	○	○	○	#4̇	#1̈	7̇	#5̇	#2̈
	●	●	●	●	●	○	5̇	2̈	1̈	6̇	3̈

Remarks: "●" as closed ; "○" as opened ; "◐" as half-closed

The fingering chart of a six-holed C-key dizi:

Blowing way / Fingering hole	Slow blowing										Fast blowing																
6th hole	●	●	●	●	●	●	●	●	○	○	●	●	●	●	●	●	●	●	●	○	○	○	○	●	●	●	●
5th hole	●	●	●	●	●	●	●	●	●	○	●	●	●	●	●	●	○	○	○	●	○	○	●	●	○	○	○
4th hole	●	●	●	●	●	●	●	●	●	●	●	●	●	●	●	○	●	●	○	●	●	○	●	○	●	●	●
3rd hole	●	●	●	●	●	○	○	●	●	●	●	●	●	●	○	○	○	○	●	●	●	●	●	●	●	●	●
2nd hole	●	●	●	◐	○	○	○	○	○	○	●	●	◐	○	○	○	●	○	◐	●	○	●	◐	●	○	○	○
1st hole	●	◐	○	○	○	○	○	○	○	○	●	◐	○	○	○	○	○	○	●	○	●	○	◐	●	●	◐	○
1 = C (All closed as 5)	5	♯5	6	♭7	7	1	♯1	2	♭3	4	♯4	5	♯5	6	♭7	7	1̇	♯1̇	2̇	♭3̇	4̇	5̇	♯5̇	6̇	♭7̇	7̇	1̈
1 = F (All closed as 2)	2	♯2	3	4	♯4	5	♯5	6	♭7	7	1̇	♯1̇	2̇	3̇	♯4̇	♯4̇	5̇	6̇	♭7̇	7̇	1̈	♯1̈	2̈	3̈	4̈	♯4̈	5̈
1 = G (All closed as 1)	1	♯1	2	♭3	4	4	♯4	5	♭6	♭6	♭7	7	1̇	♯1̇	♭3̇	♭3̇	4̇	5̇	♭6̇	♭6̇	♭7̇	1̈	♯1̈	2̈	♯1̈	3̈	4̈
1 = B♭ (All closed as 6)	6	♯6	7	1	♯1	2	♯2	3	4	♯4	5	♯5	6	♯6	7̇	1̇	♯1̇	2̇	3̇	4̇	5̇	5̇	♯5̇	6̇	7̇	♯1̈	2̈
1 = E♭ (All closed as 3)	3	4	♯4	5	♯5	6	♭6	7	1̇	♯1̇	2	♯2	3	♯4	2̇	♯4̇	5̇	♯5̇	6̇	7̇	1̈	♯1̈	2̈	3̈	4̈	5̈	6̈

Remarks: " ● " as closed ; " ○ " as opened ; " ◐ " as half-closed

The fingering chart of a six-holed E-key dizi:

Blowing way	1st hole	2nd hole	3rd hole	4th hole	5th hole	6th hole	1 = E (All closed as 5)	1 = A (All closed as 2)	1 = B (All closed as 1)	1 = D (All closed as 6)	1 = G (All closed as 3)
Slow blowing	●	●	●	●	●	●	5↓	2	1	6↓	3↓
	◐	●	●	●	●	●	#5↓	#2	#1	#6↓	4
	○	●	●	●	●	●	6↓	3	2	7↓	#4/#5
	○	◐	●	●	●	●	7↓	4	3	1	5↓
	○	○	●	●	●	●	7↓	#4	3	2↓	#5↓/6
	○	○	○	●	●	●	1	5↓	4	2	6↓/#6
	○	○	○	○	●	●	#1	#5↓	#4	#2	7↓
	○	○	●	●	○	●	2	6↓	5↓	3	1
	○	○	○	●	●	○	#2	#6↓	#5↓	4	#1
	○	○	○	○	○	●	3	7↓	6↓	#4	2
	○	○	○	○	○	○	4	1	7↓	5	#2
Fast blowing	○	○	○	○	○	◐	#4	#1	7↓	#5	#2
	●	●	●	●	●	○	5	2	1	6	3
	◐	●	●	●	●	●	#5	#2	#1	#6	4
	○	●	●	●	●	●	6	3	2	7	#4
	○	◐	●	●	●	●	7	4	3↑	1↑	5
	○	○	●	●	●	●	7	#4	3↑	#1↑	#5
	○	○	○	●	●	●	1↑	5	4↑	2↑	6
	○	○	○	○	●	●	#1↑	#5	#4↑	#2↑	#6
	○	○	○	○	○	●	2↑	6	5↑	3↑	7
	○	○	○	○	◐	●	#2↑	#6	#5↑	4↑	7
	○	○	○	○	○	●	3↑	7	6↑	#4↑	1↑
	●	●	●	●	●	○	4↑	1↑	7↑	5↑	#1↑
	○	○	○	●	○	○					
	○	◐	●	○	○	○	#4↑	#1↑	7↑	#5↑	#2↑
	●	●	●	●	●	○	5↑	2↑	1↑	6↑	3↑
	○	○	○	●	○	○					
	◐	●	●	◐	●	●	#5↑	#2↑	#1↑	#6↑	4↑
	○	●	●	○	●	●	6↑	3↑	2↑	7↑	#4↑
	◐	◐	●	◐	○	●	7↑	4↑	3↑	1↑	5↑
	●	●	●	●	○	●					
	●	○	●	●	○	●					
	○	○	○	●	○	●	1↑	5↑	4↑	2↑	6↑

Remarks: "●" as closed ; "○" as opened ; "◐" as half-closed

Maintenance of the Dizi

Maintenance is essential for all musical instruments to endure their usable life. Though the price of a dizi is not comparable with those of other Chinese musical instruments such as the erhu/二胡, the pipa/琵琶, and the yangqin/揚琴, it is still worth carrying out proper maintenance in view of the difficulty in finding a suitable dizi.

The dizi, like other musical instruments, should be stored in a cool place with good ventilation, where it is not directly exposed to the sun and rain. Remember that whenever we finish playing the dizi, we should wipe the interior of the dizi with a long stick wrapped by a piece of clean cloth to remove the moisture inside, and place it in its case afterwards.

We can also use a brush to clean the interior of the dizi

The membrane will become flaccid or tightened subject to changes in the humidity of the surrounding environment. In both cases, we can re-adjust the elasticity of the membrane in the following ways:

If the membrane is too flaccid, we can press all the six finger holes with our fingers and cover the blowing hole with our mouth. Blow warm air into the dizi and the membrane will slowly contract.

If the membrane is too tightened, we can blow air onto the membrane for several times and the membrane will slowly relax.

If the dizi is out of tune, we can rectify it by several means, including:

1) If the octaves of the dizi are lower than the actual ones, we can screw the copper joint or push the stopper plug toward the blowing hole; otherwise, we can unscrew the copper joint or push the stopper plug toward the head;

2) If the pitch of the dizi is relatively lower on average, we can shift the blowing hole toward the tail by scooping out a bit of its edge toward the tail with a sharp knife, and concurrently sealing a bit of its edge toward the head with yellow wax. If the pitch of the dizi is relatively higher on average, we can do the other way round; and

3) The aforesaid method can also be applied to a specific finger hole if the relevant note is not correct. Shift the finger hole toward the tail if the pitch is lower, or toward the head if the pitch is higher. We have to keep in mind that the size of the holes must remain roughly the same before and after their displacement on the body. The amount of edges scooped out should be equal to that of the yellow wax filled.

Yellow wax

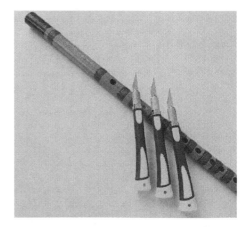

Knifes designated for scooping dizis

In a nutshell, the pitch will become higher if we decrease the acoustic length of the dizi, and vice versa.

If it is difficult to produce high notes, we can trim the periphery of the blowing hole to make it blunter, adjust the fundamental tone holes, or modify the inner diameter of the body at the tail.

If there is air leakage at the head, we can replace the worn stopper plug with a new one that can be easily purchased on the Internet at a low price less than USD 0.2 (like the corks shown in the right picture).

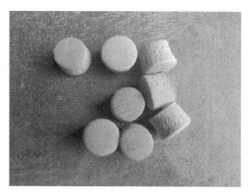

If the overtones are out of tune, there are already intrinsic problems with the dizi in term of its inner diameter or spacing of the holes, which are unable to be fixed unfortunately.   In this case, we have no choice but to buy another dizi.

The answers for the quiz on Pages 32 ~ 33 are:
1. The solfeggio " 1 ";
2. The solfeggio " 3 ";
3. The solfeggio " 6 ";
4. The solfeggio " 5 ";
5. The solfeggio " 2 ".

Selected Songs

After going through all these chapters, let's play some simple songs and apply the things we have learnt so far!

青春舞曲

The Dance of Youth

1 = F (All closed as 5) 2/4   Xinjiang Folk Song

3 2 7 1 | 3 2 1 7 | 6   6 4 | 3   - | 3 2 7 1 | 3 2 1 7 | 6   6 6 |

6   0 | 6 7 1 2 | 3   6 4 | 3   3 2 | 3   - | 3 2 7 1 | 3 2 1 7 |

6   6 4 | 3   - | 3 2 7 1 | 3 2 1 7 | 6   6 6 | 6   - | 6 7 1 7 |

1   7 6 | 7 1 7 6 | 7   - | 7 1 2 4 | 3 2 1 7 | 6   6 6 | 6 tr   -   ‖

康定情歌

Kangding Love Song

1 = F (C/F Bangdi, all closed as 5) 2/4   Sichuan Folk Song

Moderato, con expressione

3 5   6 6 5 | 6·3   2 ᵛ| 3 5   6 6 5 | 6 3· ᵛ| 3 5   6 6 5 | 6·3   2 ᵛ|

decelerando

5 3   2321 | 2 6· ᵛ| 6 2· | 5 3· | 2 1 6· ᵛ‖: 5 3   2321 | [1] 2 6· | [2] 2 6· ‖

老六版

Lao Liu Ban

1 = D (all closed as 5) 2/4

♩ = 80

Folk Song

```
3 3   6 2 | 1      5 6 | 1     6 1 | 1 3   2   | 3 3   6 2 | 1      5 6 |
1     3 2 | 1 6    5   | 5 5   3 3 | 5 5   2   | 3 2   1 1 | 6 1    2   |
3 2   2 3 | 5      5 6 | 1     6 1 | 1 6   5   | 5 6   5 3 | 2      2 3 |
5     5 6 | 5 3   2   | 2 5   5 2 | 3 2   1   | 6 1   5 6 | 1 3    2   |
2 5   5 2 | 3 2   1   | 3 3   6 2 | 1      5 6 | 1     3 2 | 1 6    5   ‖
```
rit

鳳陽花鼓

Feng Yang Flower Drum

1 = F (all closed as 5) 2/4

Anhui Folk Song

```
6     6 5 | 3 .  5 | 6     6 5 | 3     -  v | 3 2   3 5 | 6 5   6 i | 6 5   3 1 |
2     -  v | 1 6   1 2 | 3     5 | 3     2 1 | 2     -  v | 6     6 5 | 3 5   6 i |
6 5   3   | 2     -  v | 3     3 3 | 2     0 | 3     3 3 | 2     0 | 3     3 3 |
2 3   2 3 | 2     2 3 | 2     -  v | 6     6 5 | 6     i   | 2     i 6 | 5     -  v |
6 v   6 5 | 3     i | 6     5 3 | 2     -  v | 1 .  2 | 3     5 | 3     2 1 |
2     -  v | 6     6 5   3 5 | 6 i   6 5 | 3     2 | 2     -  v | 3     3 3 | 2     0 |
3     3 3 | 2     0 | 3     3 3 | 2 3   2 3 | 2     2 3 | 2     -  ‖
```

嘎達梅林

Gada Meiren

1 = F (all closed as 2̣) 4/4

Inner Monogolian Folk Song

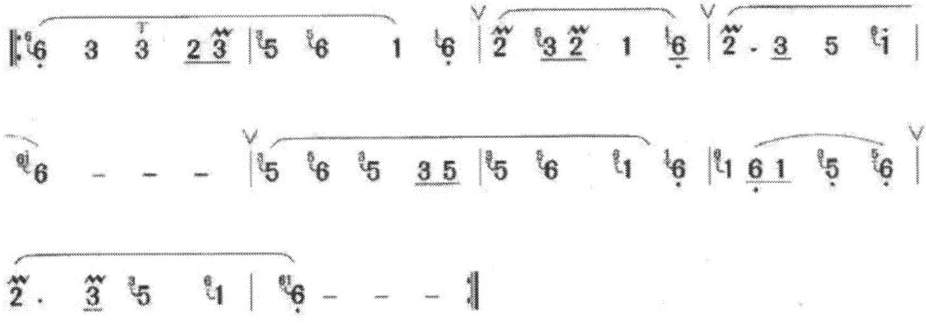

瀏陽河

Liuyang River

1 = D (all closed as 5̣) 2/4

Moderato

Hunan Folk Song

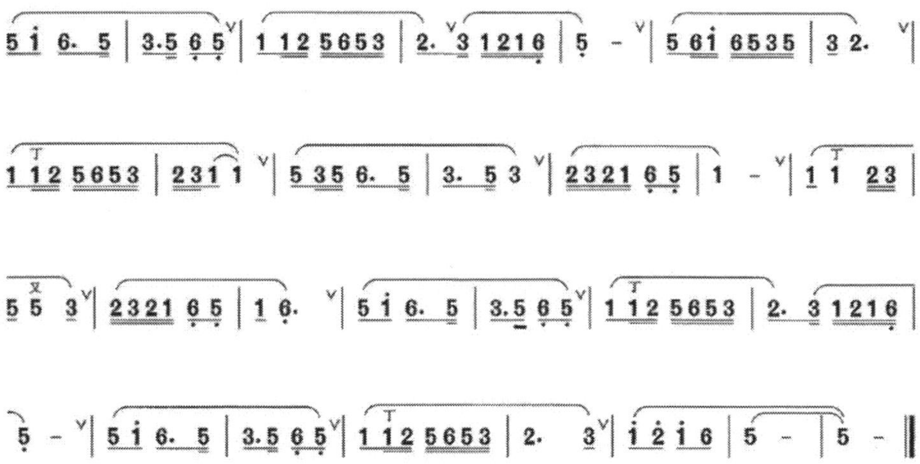

八段錦

Eight Pieces of Brocade

1 = G (all closed as 5)

Folk Song

$\frac{4}{4}$ 1 1 2 1 | 65 61 5 - | 56 12 65 3 | 52 35 1 - |

35 61 5. 6 | 35 61 5 - | 56 12 65 3 | 52 35 1 - |

32 13 2. 5 | 32 13 2 - | 56 12 65 3 | 52 35 1 - ‖

采茶撲蝶

Picking Tea and Chasing Butterflies

1 = D (all closed as 5) $\frac{2}{4}$

Fujian Folk Song

Moderato

5 65 32 | 1 1 2 | 1 3 2 | 1 6 1 21 | 6 - ‖: 6 5 | 3 5 65 |

6. 5 6 | 6. 1 5 | 3 6 5 2 | 3 2 3 | 6. 1 5 | 3 5 65 | 6. 5 6 |

6. 1 5 | 3 6 5 2 | 3. 2 3 | 6. 5 6 | 3. 2 3 | 3 5 35 | 5 3 2 |

1 6 1 | 2 - | 5 65 32 | 1 1 2 | 1 3 2 | 1 6 1 21 | 6 - ‖

Fine

1 = G (all closed as 2)

‖: 3 3 5 32 | 1 3 2 | 5 32 1 61 | 2 - | 1 3 2 | 1 6 1 21 | 6 - |

1 6 1 2 | 3 - | 5 32 1 61 | 2 - | 1 3 2 | 1 6 1 21 | 6 - ‖

D. S.

50

茉莉花

Jasmine Flower

1 = D （all closed as 5）

Jiangsu Folk Song

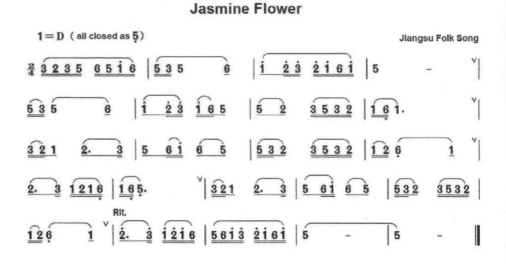

蘇武牧羊

Su Wu Herding Sheep

1 = D （all closed as 5）

Moderato

Ancient song

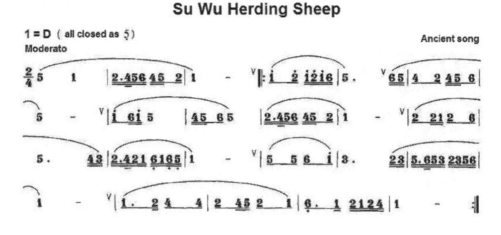

Purple Bamboo Melody

1 = D (all closed as 5) $\frac{2}{4}$

Moderato

Jiangnan Folk Song

(6 5 6 1 2 1 7 | 6 7 6 5 3 2 3 5 | 6 0 6 0) | 6 5 6 1 5 6 5 3 | 6 5 6 1 5 6 5 3 |

2 3 5 1 6 5 3 2 | 1. 6 5 3 1 6 5 | 3 2 3 5 6 5 6 1 | 5. 5 6 |

3 2 3 5 6 5 6 1 | 5. 5 6 1 7 6 5 3 5 6 1 | 5. 5 6 5 6 5 1 7 |

6 7 6 5 3 5 2 3 | 5 6 5 2 3 5 3 2 | 1. 6 5 | 1 6 1 2 5 6 5 3 | 2 3 2 1 2 |

3 5 1 6 5 3 2 | 1. 2 7 6 5 | 6. 7 6 5 3 2 | 1 6 1 2 5 6 5 3 | 2 3 2 1 2 |

3. 5 6 5 3 2 | 1. 2 7 6 5 | 6 - | 6 5 6 1 5 6 5 3 | 6 5 6 1 5 6 5 3 |

2 3 5 1 6 5 3 2 | 1. 1 2 3 1 | 6 5 3 2 3 5 6 5 6 1 | 5. 5 6 |

3 2 3 5 6 5 6 1 | 5. 5 6 1 7 6 5 3 5 6 1 | 5. 5 6 5 6 5 1 7 |

6 7 6 5 3 5 2 3 | 5 6 5 2 3 5 3 2 | 1. 6 5 | 1 6 1 2 5 6 5 3 | 2 3 2 1 2 | 3 5 1 6 5 3 2 |

1. 2 7 6 5 | 6. 7 6 5 3 2 | 1 6 1 2 5 6 5 3 | 2 3 2 1 2 | 3 5 5 6 | 1. 2 7 6 5 6 - ‖

Slightly Opening the Door

1 = G (all closed as 5)

Folk Song

0 0 0 3 5 | 6 1 6 5 3 5 2 6 | 1 - - 3 5 | 6. 5 6 6 |

‖: 0 3 5 3 5 6 | 1. 2 6 5 3 | 0 5 6 6 5 | 3 5 2 3 - |

3 0 2 3 5. 1 | 6 1 6 5 3 5 2 6 | 1 - - 2 3 | 6 6 1 5 6 |

1 - - 2 | 3 6 1 2 | 3 - - 5 | 6 3 5 6 |

1. 3 2 3 1 | 0 2 1 5 | 6. 5 6 6 | 6 3 5 6 | 5 - - - ‖

52

句句雙

Ju Ju Shuang

1 = G （all closed as 5）

```
2/4 ‖: 5.  6 5 6 | i 6   5      | 2 5   5 32 | 3 6   1    :‖ 5 6   5    |

216   1       | 5 6   5      | 216   1      | 3 5   5 32 | 1 3   2    |

3 5   5 32 | 1 6   2      | 6 2   i 6    | 5 3   5    | 5.  6 5 6  |

i 6   i       | 5 i   i i i | i i   3      | 3 6   5 32 | 6 1   2    |

3 5   5 32 | 3 6   1      | 216   1      | 216   1    | 2 1   2 1  |

216   1       | 2 5   5 32 | 3 5   1      ‖: 5.  6 5 6 | i 6   5    |

235   5 32 | 3 6   1      ‖: i 6 i   5  | 216   1    | i 6 i   5  |

216   1       | 3 2 3 5   6 i 6 5 | 1 3   2   | 3 2 3 5   6 i 6 5 | 1 3   2 |

6 2   i 6   | 5 6   5      | 5.  6 5 6  | i 6 5 6   i  | 5 6 i   6 i 6 5 |

3 5 3 2   3 | 3 5 6 i   5 3 | 2 1   2   | 2 3 5   5 32 | 3 6   1    |

2 6   1       | 2 6   1      | 2 1   2 1  | 216   1    | 2 5   5 32 | 3 6   1 ‖
```

53

快樂頌

Ode to Joy

1 = C (All closed as 2) $\frac{4}{4}$

Ludwig van Beethoven

Moderato

| 3 3 4 5 | 5 4 3 2 | 1 1 2 3 | 3. 2 2 - |

| 3 3 4 5 | 5 4 3 2 | 1 1 2 3 | 2. 1 1 - |

| 2 - 3 1 | 2 3 4 3 1 | 2 3 4 3 2 | 1 2 5 3 |

| 3 3 4 5 | 5 4 3 2 | 1 1 2 3 | 2. 1 1 - |

| 2. 1 1 2 3 4 5 | 3 3 4 5 | 5 4 3 2 | 1 1 2 3 |

| 3. 2 2 - | 3 3 4 5 | 5 4 3 2 | 1 1 2 3 |

| 2. 1 1 - | 2 - 3 1 | 2 3 4 3 1 | 2 3 4 3 2 |

| 1 2 5 3 | 3 3 4 5 | 5 4 3 2 | 1 1 2 3 |

| 2. 1 1 - | rit. 1 1. 1 2 3 | 2. 1 1 - |

魔笛

The Magic Flute

1 =E (All closed as 5) 4/4

Wolfgang Amadeus Mozart

Allegretto

(5 4 | 3 5 1 3 5 3 | 4 6 2 4 6 4 | 3 5 1 2 4 7 | 1 3 1) 5 4 |

3 1 3 5 3 | 4 2 4 4 3 | 2 7 2 7 | 1 3 1 3 1 5 4 |

3 5 1 3 5 3 | 4 6 2 4 6 4 | 3 5 1 2 4 7 | 1 3 1 5 4 |

3 3 0 3 | 4 4 0 4 3 | 2 2 0 2 | 3 - 0 5 4 |

3 - 3 3 | 4. 5 6 4 | 3 - 2. 2 | 1 - 0 4 3 |

2 2 0 2 | 3 3 0 3 | 4 0 4. 5 | 3 - 0 3 4 |

5 - 5 5 | 6. 7 1 4 | 3 - 2. 2 | 1 - 0 4 3 |

2 2 0 2 | 3 3 0 3 | 4 0 4. 5 | 3 - 0 3 4 |

5 - 5 5 | 6. 7 1 4 | 3 - 2. 2 | 1 - 0 |

D.C.

D.C. = *Da capo* (an Italian term literally meaning "from the head"), which tells us to repeat the whole song from the beginning.

那不勒斯舞曲

Online Materials

The following YouTube video clips feature the performance of the dizi master LU Chunlin/陸春齡 (1921 ~ 2018), nicknamed "the magic flute" for his consummate and splendid skills in playing the dizi:

https://www.youtube.com/watch?v=vNcMOzfDesI&list=PLED641ED4DC3C7892